# Falling For Work:
## A Story of Death and Determination

by
Kimberly Messer

ISBN: 978-1-329-45856-7

In memory of all workers whose deaths may have been prevented, and in honor of the professionals who work tirelessly to improve workplace safety.

# Foreword

Proper execution of your fall protection program means the difference between life and death for workers at heights.

In this story, a fatality is the catalyst for investing in a managed fall protection program. It doesn't have to be that way. Managing the major risks presented by falls is a smart and ethical business investment, as well as a legal requirement.

Overall fall fatalities and the associated costs are increasing, despite the fact that the amount of money spent on personal protective equipment has doubled. The challenge of fall protection is complex. There are numerous regulations, standards, equipment options, training sources and priorities. Plus, fall protection presents two conflicting realities: significant fall incidents don't happen often, but when they do occur, they're catastrophic and costly. Unfortunately, the rarity of accidents can lull both management and workers into a false sense of security. It can be expensive and deadly to assume it won't happen in your organization.

Since 2006 I have been working with Kimberly to help educate organizations about the risk of falls, and ways to reduce those risks. Although she doesn't have a safety or engineering background, she quickly grasped the concepts we promote and developed a passion for protecting workers at heights. She puts her communication skills to work to articulate the critical messages that sometimes get lost amongst details on regulations and technology.

When she developed the idea for this book, I was amazed at

how much she understood about the complexities, nuances and challenges of fall protection—and how well she simplified the concepts. Many elements of this story were adapted from real-world scenarios faced during LJB's consulting work. In the past, I have struggled to tell our stories and pass on lessons learned in a convincing, compelling way. Kimberly captures the essence of effective fall protection through this parable and these characters. For that, I thank her on behalf of my colleagues at LJB, our partners in the industry, and the organizations that this story will benefit.

I resonate with Dan's character in this book in many ways. I got involved with fall protection to improve the quality of life for our clients. I didn't have a personal connection to someone who fell, but I quickly learned the impact my fall protection design work could have.

My passion for fall protection was solidified on Memorial Day weekend 1998. The Friday before the holiday weekend, I received a call saying a horizontal lifeline I had helped design saved a worker's life at a construction site. The magnitude to which my work could impact a person, a family and an organization hit home that day.

While that story had a happy ending, Steve's character in this book isn't so lucky. His organization was ignorant about fall protection and unprepared to properly address the significant risk of falls.

I hear these sentiments every day: fall protection is too difficult, the regulations are confusing and it's expensive. All these things are true, but that doesn't change the fact that workers need to be protected.

You aren't alone in trying to tackle the fall protection issue. Find help to protect your workers at heights. You can get help from industry associations, OSHA, consultants and equipment manufacturers. You can invest in training to better educate your people.

As this book illustrates, when fall protection issues are properly addressed, the result is increased safety and reduced risk. But, it isn't easy, and the work is never finished. Fall protection requires a synthesis of structural engineering and safety disciplines. Structural engineering addresses the physical strength and performance of fall protection systems, while safety engineering focuses on the behavioral aspects. Designs that consider only one point of view tend to result in systems that are uneconomical, unworkable and often unsafe.

An effective program will reflect a deep understanding of the governing regulations. In the United States, OSHA regulations are the law, but they are severely outdated and limited, since they have to apply to such a broad audience. For current best practices, many organizations turn to the ANSI Z359 fall protection consensus standards for guidance.

As the characters in this book learn, fall protection isn't always easy to tackle, but it's certainly worth the effort. Thank you for taking the time to learn about this critical safety subject. As the narrator Dan learns about fall protection, I hope you also glean useful points to apply to your fall protection program.

Our goal is to eliminate stories like Steve's from the workplace. By learning and working together, we can reduce risk for workers at heights and make sure no family has to endure the pain of losing someone to a preventable accident.

Thomas E. Kramer, P.E., C.S.P.
Managing Principal, LJB Inc.
President, International Society for Fall Protection
Vice Chair, ANSI Z359 Committee on Fall Protection

## Chapter 1

# It Really Matters

Even though it takes a few extra minutes in the morning, I take the long way to my desk these days. I know exactly where my best friend and co-worker died. Even though it happened months ago, I still think of him every time I walk through that part of the plant.

Steve slipped as he loosened a bolt on an old piece of equipment. He fell 12 feet to his death. I wasn't there to see it, thank God, but everyone who did said it happened so quickly. One minute Steve was working as usual. The next he lay broken on the concrete floor.

Steve and I had plans to go fishing a few weeks after the accident. Instead, I helped his 30-year-old widow, Angela, sort through their garage. At the time, I wished I could have done more for her. I couldn't imagine losing your spouse so unexpectedly. I couldn't imagine how to explain this to two little girls who just want their daddy to come home.

After the accident, I blamed everyone. I blamed God for allowing this to happen. I blamed Steve's work partner for not doing something to stop it. I blamed LMK Industries for not doing more to protect workers like me and Steve and hundreds more like us.

Then I grew angry at myself. I knew we weren't really protected when we had to work up on equipment. The fall protection class I took taught me that. For a while I thought about doing something about it. I even said something to my supervisor, Ted, but it went nowhere and I let it go. No one had ever fallen before. Falls seemed unlikely. Shows what I knew.

I thought I was invincible, and I didn't want to be "that guy" — the one that harps on safety stuff.

I had no business being that guy. I wore my steel-toed shoes and my hard hat, but I was just like the other guys when it came to fall protection gear. I avoided using it. I'm sure I didn't wear it right. I didn't like the feel of the tight harness when an equipment rep had me try it on. Now, though, I'd wear a straitjacket if I knew it would save my life.

My wife, Cheryl, let me vent my anger and frustration for a couple of weeks. Finally, she said something that got me thinking.

"Dan, if you aren't part of the solution, you're part of the problem," Cheryl said in her best honey-I-love-you-but-you-need-to-hear-this voice. There's a reason why people call her my better half.

Still, I wasn't ready to hear it. I just wanted to wallow in my grief and stay mad at the world. Why would I do anything extra for a company that killed my best friend?

Slowly, I realized what Cheryl said might be true. Maybe this accident was what LMK needed to focus on employee safety.

Maybe I could take action and make sure something good came of Steve's awful death.

I was sure my supervisor, Ted, and other managers would be feeling some pressure to do something to improve fall safety. I was sure they didn't like having OSHA — the federal Occupational Safety and Hazard Administration — poking around, dealing with insurance, or answering questions from the press. And I knew they REALLY didn't want to face Steve's wife and kids.

It was too late to save Steve, but maybe I could start a movement in Steve's honor that would save someone else's life, including mine. Maybe LMK could be a model for fall protection safety. It was worth a shot.

## Chapter 2

# It's a Program – Not a Project

After spending the weekend with Steve's family, I became more motivated than ever to approach management about addressing fall protection.

I knew it would be difficult to sort through Steve's belongings, and I teared up when I found a piece of old camping equipment in the garage. It was even harder to hear Angela tell stories about trips she and Steve had taken and projects they had started. Before I left, though, I heard what I wanted to hear.

Despite plans not to, I told Angela about my idea of approaching company management about fall protection. I threw it out there while we were sorting hand tools, just to hear her reaction. She blew up and blamed LMK for not having more safeguards in place, cursed the company for negligence and stormed off, saying she needed some air. Maybe it was too soon for her to think something positive could come from Steve's death.

When Angela came back, she said no more about it and we set about our work again. Maybe this wasn't a good idea, I thought, "Maybe this is all too fresh and personal for me, too. Can I really objectively look at what the company needs to do?"

A few hours later, as we sorted through the last of the stuff in the garage, Angela quietly said, "You should do it."

We had been working in near silence so long I had to ask her to repeat it.

"You should do it. I want you to talk to management," she said. "I don't want someone else to just get *an assignment*," she said with a sneer. "If someone is going to use this — the death of my husband — to make a change, it should be you. I want it to be someone who really cares about this, someone who cared about Steve and wants to make sure no other family has to go through this."

Angela's words played over and over in my head that night: "If someone is going to use this — the death of my husband — to make a change, it should be you." How could I not follow through now? I at least had to try.

I was full of resolve, but I didn't get a chance to bring it up to Ted on Monday. Maybe I could have forced the issue, but I wanted to have his full attention. My opportunity came on Tuesday afternoon.

Ted called me in for a status report on a project. After we addressed the business at hand, I asked for a few more minutes to talk about Steve's death. At first, Ted looked apprehensive, like I was going to ask for therapy or something. He knew Steve and I were close, so I think he was anxious about what I might say. He seemed somewhat reluctant to talk about it, but I think he was also afraid to put me off, so I started right in.

"Ted, is there a plan to address the fall protection issues? I know the company has to be talking about it, considering all the attention surrounding Steve's death."

He seemed a little relieved this was a company issue he could address.

"Well, Dan, I wouldn't say there's a solid plan, but there is a movement to do something," he said. "I mean, we have to do something or we'll be in more trouble with OSHA."

Not exactly a proactive plan, but at least it was a start. They knew they should do something, even if it was for business reasons.

"Has someone been assigned to work on it yet?" I said.

"Not yet," Ted said. "Right now, we're thinking about assigning Mark to get some anchor points or something installed at the location of the fall and put everyone through some more training."

"Is that the extent of the plans?" I said, trying to hide my disgust that they were just going to address the obvious issue but ignore everything else that was woefully lacking in our fall protection program.

I think Ted sensed my feelings despite my effort to mask them.

"No one really has an obvious desire or expertise in that area, and you know how busy all the safety professionals are," Ted said. "It's tough to figure out who could carve out time to deal with this. Frankly, we don't even know what else we could or should be doing."

"What if I have a desire, a desire to do this right?" I said. "I really don't think dealing with one location is what we need. That's a project that'll be handled by just a few people and will affect only a few people. I think the company needs to do more to show a commitment to the safety of workers throughout the plant."

Ted didn't look convinced, but he listened.

"I know I was hired to be a millwright, but what if I commit to understanding fall protection and recommending a program for the whole company?" I said. "I really think that's what LMK needs to do to show the staff, the community and OHSA it's genuinely working to improve."

I paused, partly because I could see Ted processing and partly because I was getting emotional.

"I really want to do this," I said. "I want to do this for Steve and his family."

Ted thought for a moment and responded as I suspected he would.

"I don't know how upper management would react to this," he said. "A program sounds like a lot of time and money. You know how Derek in operations is. He's already pushing for us to implement a quick fix on this and move on to 'more important' things. I know the company generally wants to do the right thing here, but would we be biting off more than we could chew or management could swallow?"

"Right now, we don't know what we don't know," I said. "I can't tell you how much time and money it would take. But I've come up with a plan for how to carve out 10 hours a week to work on this issue so we can get a better understanding of this. I'm no safety expert, but I'd like to put my plan out there for management to consider."

We talked a bit more, and Ted agreed to bring up the idea in his meeting with management that Friday.

Although I tried not to get my hopes up, I was anxious all day Friday, wondering what management would say — especially Derek, the naysayer in the group. I wasn't confident Ted would carry the message as strongly as I would, at least enough to convince someone like Derek. Just as I started to forget about it, Ted found me and asked me to join the management team meeting.

This seemed like a good sign, but I panicked. I remember thinking, "I'm not prepared for whatever they might throw at me. I wasn't planning on presenting anything today. What if I don't seem credible enough to take this on? Is this the beginning of the end? What would I tell Angela?"

Thankfully, it wasn't the gauntlet I had imagined. They just had lots of questions for me. Some were about fall protection, some were about my role and current projects and some were even about Steve. I could tell Derek wasn't the only person looking for reasons not to do this. But I could also tell one or two people agreed when I said we needed a coordinated program throughout the company—not just a quick fix.

Although I didn't get an answer about moving forward, I felt encouraged when I left the meeting. At least I had an opportunity to bring up issues about worker training, fall risk throughout the plant and my perceptions about the general safety culture. Who knew what would come of it, but I felt like I did what my wife, Angela, and Steve would have wanted. I made the managers aware of some problems and expressed interest in making it better for the whole company for the long term.

The next week, I went about my day job and tried not to think too much about the meeting. But as the week went on, I found myself getting more discouraged. As I prepared to leave work that Friday afternoon, Ted approached me, but I couldn't read his expression.

"Dan, I've just come from the management team meeting and we'd like you to move forward in defining a fall protection program. I will be honest and tell you only some of the group is supportive of this program, especially until they know more about what it will take."

I could already guess who the unsupportive people were, but I felt buoyed because their opposition obviously did not kill the idea.

"We are authorizing you to look into it and provide a recommendation for a program," Ted said. "For now, though,

Mark is going to address the area. You know — the area where Steve fell."

Ted explained they wanted the fall investigated and dealt with by someone who wasn't so close to the issue. They knew the OSHA investigation could be detailed and time-consuming, and they were concerned I couldn't be objective in developing solutions. I understood that logic, but it still seemed like they were just going to throw a Band-Aid on the situation. I didn't think I could change their minds on this one.

Before we left for the weekend, Ted and I talked about the expectations and deadlines for my recommendations on the program.

As I left that day, I purposely walked past the scene of Steve's fall. Even though I wouldn't be directly addressing this spot, I was going to get the chance to do something for him. I looked up toward the sky and promised to do everything I could to make this happen.

"Now, if only I knew where to begin," I thought.

# Chapter 3

# Do you know what you don't know?

Although I had no idea where to start, I grew excited about the opportunity to sink my teeth into the fall protection issue. When I told Cheryl about it that night, she suggested we tell Angela about it in person that weekend. I was a little apprehensive since I didn't know where all this would lead, but Cheryl convinced me any good news would be helpful for Angela.

We invited Angela and the kids to a picnic dinner the next night. Once the kids were off playing, I told Angela about the direction I got from management. She thanked me, then asked a ton of questions, most of which I couldn't answer. I promised I would find answers and keep her posted about our progress. With that business out of the way, we enjoyed the evening as friends, just like we used to. Well, almost. We all missed Steve's presence.

While Cheryl and the kids were out the next day, I sat down at the computer. I figured when you don't know where else to turn, there's always the Internet. I knew I needed to get my hands on whatever documents we had at the office, but I was eager to do something immediately.

I found plenty of information about fall protection on the Internet. I found a ton of sites that sold equipment. I also found some information on regulations and standards and some on fall protection training. I started taking some notes because the information was all over the place.

When Cheryl and the kids got home, I told her about what I had found and confessed I was in over my head.

"I never knew it was so complicated," I told her. "Maybe this is why we haven't been doing it right at work. It's just too confusing, especially when you're starting from nothing."

I decided to let it go for the day and to regroup once I could get whatever we had at work.

The first thing I did the next morning was find my old training binder from the fall protection class I took a few years ago. I had not touched it since I took the class. The dust on the top told me I was as guilty as anyone about failing to make this a priority.

Next, I went to the safety office and found my buddy Pete. I had known Pete for several years, and I hoped he would be an ally. I was really hoping the folks in the safety office didn't take offense to my involvement.

"Hey Pete," I said. "Long time, no see, old friend."

"Well, Dan, how's it going? I haven't seen you in a while," Pete said. "Dan, I've been meaning to come talk to you. I'm sorry about Steve. I know you guys were friends."

"Thanks, Pete," I replied. "That's sort of what I'm here to talk to you about."

That seemed to throw him off guard a little, so I quickly launched into a description of my new part-time safety role. Pete looked relieved that it was a work issue, not a personal one.

"Dan, this is great—having someone committed to addressing fall protection," Pete said. "Especially now. I know it's important and I've been pulled in a little bit, but I'm swamped as it is."

I was so glad Pete welcomed my help and seemed happy to have someone else take this on. I could worry less about stepping on toes and more on getting something accomplished.

First, Pete showed me copies of the regulations and standards we had on file. It seemed like the regulations were old, although some of the standards were newer. Pete also gave me a copy of the entire safety program document, which included a section on fall protection. Pete admitted he wasn't "a fall protection guy," but at least he knew some things I could use and where they were. That was a start.

I was overwhelmed with what I had found online, and the stacks of paperwork Pete produced had me reeling. Luckily, I had my day job to do, so I could focus on that for a while. I still felt unsure. At least I had started. My plan was to read everything. I wanted to know if our current program at least met the regulations and standards, even if the program wasn't being implemented or enforced.

When I dove deeper into the documents, I became more confused. Pete had given me OSHA 1910 regulations, but they were published more than 40 years ago. There were also other OSHA documents that mentioned fall protection. Then I found other documents that referenced OSHA 1926 regulations. I remembered seeing that mentioned in my Internet research, but it wasn't in our program and I didn't have a copy. I made a note to find out about that.

I also pulled out standards from the American National Standards Institute (ANSI). Some were a little dated, but not as old as the OSHA regulations. There seemed to be a lot of information about equipment.

I struck gold when I read the ANSI Z359.2 standard, one of the more current resources Pete had given me. It had an entire section on managed fall protection programs. In a sea of confusion, it felt like a beacon of hope. The standard described the key elements of what it called "a comprehensive managed fall protection program." That sounded like fancy words for doing fall protection the right way, but I still felt like I had found the key.

When I checked the ANSI program recommendations against LMK's program, I learned we had done a few things right but were missing a lot of things and not enforcing others. The Z359.2 standard was also closely aligned to OSHA's five core elements of a safety program, so I felt good about that consistency. I took a step back and thought about each of the core elements and what our plant was doing for each.

The first one, **management leadership and employee participation**, was clearly not a strong point. We had no fall protection program to speak of, and it seemed like management was only involved and interested right now because of the accident. Still, we had a safety department with a budget. My experience with employee participation in safety activities was minimal and half-hearted at best. This element definitely needed improvement.

The next element, **hazard identification and evaluation**, focused on knowing where workers encountered risk and evaluating options to mitigate risk. My view was probably short-sighted and biased, but we clearly didn't identify the fall risk at the site of Steve's accident. That alone was enough to give us a failing grade for this element.

**Hazard abatement** was the next element. Although I didn't know a lot about this, I was aware of some fall protection equipment and solutions like aerial lifts. But, I also didn't have much confidence that they were appropriate, used correctly or in good shape for effective use.

The **training** element was at least one that I had firsthand experience with. Judging by my lack of knowledge and ability to apply anything I learned, I can only assume many other workers are the same way. I can barely remember anything from that training, except how boring it was. Even though we have had some training, I can't consider this a successful or effective element either.

The last element, **program evaluation**, was all about continuous improvement. Do we regularly evaluate how effective our fall protection is? What fall protection program? Other than a cursory tool box talk, the general population of the company never talks about safety. And, no one has ever asked my opinion – not that I would have had much to say before.

I couldn't give us a passing grade on a single element. At that point, I decided to make the ANSI standard the basis for my recommendation, since it provided more detailed guidance about what our program should look like. At that point, my head was swimming and I stopped for the day.

When I had cleared my head enough to get back to it, I dug into the ANSI standards a bit more and a potential roadblock hit me. ANSI standards aren't mandatory. They're suggested industry best practices, but they aren't laws like OSHA. By digging a little deeper, though, I discovered that OSHA refers to the ANSI Z359 standards in violations that cite the General Duty clause. This clause essentially says any recognized hazard can be cited under the General Duty clause. Since the ANSI standards identify many potential fall hazards — and represent an industry standard of care — OSHA can issue a violation for not adhering to ANSI guidance.

The more I read, the more I realized ANSI had more updated information and clear direction for developing and maintaining an effective fall protection program. Required or not, following ANSI would be my recommendation.

I relished that decision as a small victory since there were still so many unknowns. After pouring through all that material, I started a list of what I needed to know. Some of the things I could investigate easily on my own or with Pete's help. Others would be larger research tasks to be done during the next step, assuming we got to a next step.

I wanted to understand the difference between OSHA 1910 and 1926. Does OSHA 1926 apply to us even though construction isn't our primary business? If so, how?

I also wanted to know who in the organization had taken fall protection training. When? And, from what organization? What were the expectations of those people? If you took me for an example, it seemed like very little.

Those questions were relatively easy to answer. A few others would be less likely to have straight answers. Do we have enough of the right equipment and how do we know? For the systems we have, are they certified for use and do they each have procedures outlined for use and rescue?

Considering why this journey started, I was pretty sure I already knew the answer to my last question: have all fall hazards at the plant been identified in any way? I can't imagine Steve encountered the only unidentified fall hazard in the plant. But, what had we identified? Anything?

After digging in to OSHA 1926 and finding out it does apply to us for construction activities, I investigated the remaining issues with Pete. One thing was certain. Our documentation about fall protection equipment, systems and training was inadequate.

Armed with this new information, I submitted a memo to the management team, recommending that we adopt the ANSI program guidelines and do more investigation. The other specific thing I felt we needed immediately was new and better training for our workers. I was surprised when I looked at the training logs and determined I was nearly as qualified as anyone to work on our program.

After the managers reviewed my recommendation, they told me to proceed with personnel training and revamping our program document. Ted said the team debated a few points, but acknowledged that a lack of focus on fall protection had hurt the company. But, they weren't prepared to overhaul the entire program.

"What did Derek have to say?" I asked Ted.

"Well, he was definitely questioning whether we should follow your recommendation or just do whatever OSHA required. Honestly, in the end, he approved your recommendations because he thought they would look good to OSHA."

Not exactly the motivation I was looking for, but a "yes" was a "yes."

Hours of surfing, digging, reading, researching and thinking got us to our first milestone in improving fall protection, but I felt it was just the tip of the iceberg. Still, I savored the small victory. One thing Steve's death taught me is that I should take advantage of every day. I decided I would take my family out to celebrate. I felt like I was making a difference.

# Chapter 4

# They can be taught

I couldn't wait to tell my co-workers that they would get to sit through another training class, I thought sarcastically. Actually, I wished it was that easy. There was a lot to do before we were ready to announce training. And I only had 10 hours a week, plus whatever piece of my free time I could muster, to put into it.

First, I had to work with our HR department to find "an appropriate training provider." When I first heard that, I took "appropriate" to mean cheap, but Ted assured me that management just wanted to know we were getting a real, impactful education for our investment. I wasn't sure how I was going to prove that.

Next, I had to figure out who needed training. I had a feeling Derek was going to challenge me every time I asked for something that cost money, so I had to justify the names on my list.

I'd been engrossed in this subject enough to realize the difference between a "competent person" and "authorized person" and how different their training needed to be. So, I looked for two different courses: one for safety management and supervisors—or competent persons—and one for everyone who actually worked at heights, which ANSI calls authorized persons. I liked that phrase. It sounded so official.

Having taken fall protection training before, I had a good idea of what not to do and I kept that in mind. I remembered how boring and seemingly irrelevant my previous training was. I knew the course I took didn't change my behavior one bit. I showed my supervisor a certificate, he checked a box, and that was that. I never remembered the regulations the instructor spewed, and I thought I already knew how to wear a harness, so I daydreamed through that part.

"So, how do we avoid repeating that waste of time?" I thought.

I made it my goal to change attitudes and behaviors about fall protection training. I didn't want people to view it as just a requirement that had to be met to keep their job. I could see people thinking things like, "We had a freak accident, and now we all have to sit through another class." I had to make sure the training wasn't just general instruction on regulations and equipment use. That stuff is important but dry.

I needed to find or develop a training class our people could embrace in a way that would relate to their jobs in the plant. Maybe we could have the trainers come to our site or at least use examples from our site so people could better relate. If I could actually see myself using the skills in my real job, I would pay more attention and think about it once I got back to work. With my last training, I came straight back to work, put the binder on the shelf and didn't give it another thought.

Actually, the next time I thought about it was after Steve's accident. Could we use Steve's fall as a case study in the training, or would that be in poor taste? Maybe when people realized life was truly on the line, they would focus more on applying what they learned when they got back to work.

The next question was how to find a trainer who could deliver all the right technical information, wasn't boring and could inspire people to change. That was a tall order, especially with our staff.

I didn't know enough about what content we would need, so I went back to the ANSI standards. Bingo! The standards spelled out exactly what content we needed for both competent and authorized person training.

Armed with that information — and my own ideas about what could make training more effective — I asked HR to help in the search for trainers. I knew my 10 hours a week probably wouldn't be enough to find the right trainer, so I gave HR a list of qualifications to look for.

I knew we wanted someone that had significant fall protection training experience – not just general safety or OSHA training experience. And, since ANSI was so clear about the content that should be in the training, I wanted to make sure that we picked someone that could demonstrate that we would learn everything ANSI recommended.

Since my past training experience left much to be desired, I asked HR to look for a company that had credentials to show they can effectively train adults. I knew that just staring at a manual or presentation slides wasn't going to cut it. Plus, I wanted some references within our industry, so I could get real feedback on what their courses were like.

HR got to work researching training providers. I didn't do any of that formal research. Instead, I got some grassroots feedback from an old acquaintance.

Pete invited me to attend a luncheon presentation on fall protection that the local chapter of a safety organization was hosting. While we were there, I asked Colin, the husband of one of my wife's co-workers, about his experience with fall protection training. He told me a great story and gave me the name of his preferred trainer.

"I feel like our training programs are paying off," Colin said. "We had a bad training experience a few years ago, when someone came in and basically read the regulations to our people. It was awful. It was only one day. It was cheap and basically a waste of time," he said.

That sounded familiar.

"So, what has changed to make it work better now?" I said.

"We did a better job of finding qualified people using a formal Request for Proposals (RFP) process the next time," Colin said. "Our people came away with a whole new appreciation of what the risks are and how to avoid them. The best part is that they started to look at their job in a whole new light. Now, workers are bringing new risks to our attention because they know more."

I was intrigued. It sounded like Colin had found a trainer who could deliver the information in an inspiring way. What he described was people changing behavior. That was exactly what I wanted to get out of training.

"I'll give you an example," Colin continued. "One person who got trained recently helped us reduce risk on an elevator project. We were getting ready to install a new elevator to go to the roof of one of our buildings. The plan called for a fan to be installed on the top of the penthouse roof and it would be accessed by a ladder periodically for maintenance."

Colin saw that I wasn't exactly following, so he spelled it out for me.

"Because of where the fan would be located, we were going to have to provide fall protection for anyone who had to access it. The employee, who had just gone through fall protection training, said, 'Hey wait a minute. Why are we putting that fan up on top where we have to climb a ladder to maintain it? Let's move the fan down to the side of this penthouse area and we can access it just by standing on the main roof.' His solution was the perfect answer, and now no one had to risk climbing a ladder."

"OK, I get it," I said. "So, he basically suggested bringing it down to a height where it wouldn't require working at height. That's great. How much do you think the training had to do with that idea?"

"All I can say is that before training, our employees didn't usually think about how to safely maintain something long term," Colin said "They were just focused with getting the immediate task at hand completed without forethought about maintenance and operations hazards. I think the training brought in a new mindset that put safety at the top of mind."

I wanted that mindset shift to happen in our plant. Colin gave me the name of the trainer they used, and I thanked him for sharing his story. When I met with HR the next week, I waited to see if they had found the same company in their research. They had, so I told them Colin's story.

We all agreed the firm seemed like a good candidate to contact, as well as a few others HR had found. We still didn't know which members of our staff we were going to train. That was the next step. We didn't want to contact potential trainers until we knew exactly what we wanted.

So, the next hurdle was figuring out who needed training and how to justify the list of names to management. I wanted it to be everyone who worked at heights, as well as anyone who managed or supervised that type of work. That would be a long list. Would that fly with management?

Over the weekend, I updated Cheryl on what I had learned and told her the next steps in the process.

"I really need to recommend a list of people to be trained, plus a training company that can give us what we need," I said. "I don't want to lose momentum, but there is a lot to decide and I want to do it right the first time. I feel like Derek is just waiting for me to do something wrong or recommend something unfounded so he can push to end this. The office gossip is that Derek is referring to my work as a 'time and money suck.' He would be all too happy to have a reason to squash it."

Cheryl listened and offered some great ideas.

"If you're going to convince Derek or anyone else in management, you have to have information," she said. "Outwork them so they can't disagree. I know it's obviously different from my work, but we use pre-tests all the time to judge how much children know. Maybe you could do something similar to see what people already know?"

I had not thought of that. I thought we would just look at who took the same lackluster training I had a few years ago and add any new employees who had to work or supervise work at heights. A pre-test was an interesting idea.

Cheryl and I talked more about it that weekend and I decided the pre-test would be worthwhile and simple enough to conduct. It was a good way to make sure we were training the right people on the right topics.

I went to HR on Monday and asked Maria, my main contact, what she thought about it.

"I feel like we're asking our people to make potentially life-and-death decisions and we need to know if they are equipped to do that," I said.

Maria liked the idea, but we agreed Derek wouldn't like spending additional time and money to figure out who was properly prepared just so we could spend more time and money on training. We realized spending a little up front could save us in the long run because we could customize training to the right people and subjects based on what the test results showed.

Plus, it might force management, even Derek, to realize we needed to better understand fall protection.

Since I suspected the pre-test — which Maria called a knowledge assessment — would indicate an even greater need for training, we decided to get the ball rolling with the potential training providers. HR created an RFP using estimated numbers of trainees and sent it out. This seemed like a significant step and I felt great.

The knowledge assessment and the RFP process happened just like we predicted. I was right about the overall lack of fall protection knowledge across all areas of the company. Although he balked a little at the cost of training, even Derek agreed that the scores were concerning. I interpreted them as downright scary, but I would take "concerning" from Derek.

We hired the same firm Colin used for training his staff. The firm's response to the RFP was excellent, and their references absolutely gushed about the training they received. Combine that with Colin's story and I was confident training would be a powerful first step in improving fall protection.

Now I was actually excited to tell my co-workers they would be taking new fall protection training. I remember looking up and thinking, "Steve, I hope you're smiling, too."

# Chapter 5

# Do you see what I see? Fall hazard risk assessment

It's funny how something can stare you in the face every day, but you don't see it until someone points it out. For our staff, training uncovered some obvious fall protection issues. Our experience with training was similar to the story Colin told me. Our people were engaged and their awareness of risk seemed to be higher once they got back to work.

Several trainees told me about risks they had seen, and some supervisors were overwhelmed with new information and ideas about how to change things. It was daunting to realize we had so many unaddressed issues, but it still felt good to know we had momentum and our safety culture was shifting.

During training, we talked a lot about ANSI's elements of a fall protection program. Although we increased our knowledge, we still had a lot of work to do. The trainers showed us you can't have an effective program without working on all elements. I knew I needed to use what I had learned to make recommendations on how to improve the rest of the program.

With so much renewed focus on finding risks, the momentum leaned toward hazard identification and evaluation. The trainers recommended a comprehensive fall hazard risk assessment. Like they said, until you know where your risks are, you can't develop an effective strategy to reduce risk.

To make sure I understood how we identified hazards, I chatted with Pete. He confirmed what I suspected about our current approach.

"Before we do a project, we conduct a JSA—oh, sorry, that's a job safety analysis for a 'newbie' like you. The JSA helps us figure out if there are any safety issues to address before the work starts," Pete said.

"OK, but how far in advance are we doing these?," I countered. "If you wait until a JSA is performed, I assume you can only implement solutions that can be done quickly and without much cost. Right? I mean, I know how much productivity and efficiency are pushed around here. When the work needs to be done, I'm guessing we can only wait so long to get the safety part figured out."

"That's probably true," Pete said. "but in my experience, we've always been able to come up with something that works. It may not be the absolute best solution for safety or budget, but it's functional. Truthfully, it usually involves using some kind of equipment."

"Let me ask you something else, Pete," I said. "I want you to be brutally honest. How good do you think we are at identifying safety hazards, either through a JSA or otherwise?"

Pete paused for a moment, unsure of how I would react. Then he said, "Average at best. For example, I still don't know how we allowed Steve to work from an unguarded platform 12 feet up with no protection. A JSA should have highlighted that the edge was unprotected and some sort of accommodation was needed. I think we just get so used to what we do that we don't see the obvious hazards. Plus, we all tend to have the 'it-won't-happen-to-me' attitude."

Based on Pete's responses and the trainer's recommendation, I leaned toward doing a proactive fall hazard risk assessment. But having an outside source come in and identify fall hazards sounded expensive. I just didn't know how expensive.

One statistic I found during my research was that a 1 million square-foot manufacturing facility can easily have 1,000 fall hazards. Although we didn't have quite 1 million square feet, we would probably have hundreds of hazards to identify and evaluate. Maybe this was the type of thing Ted was concerned about when he asked if we would be biting off more than we could chew.

Still, it would be so powerful for us to know everything about our hazards: where they were for starters, the level of risk they presented, and what we might do about them. Knowing this would help our cause with OSHA, too. We had no information about where our hazards were, let alone what to do about them. The examples the trainers showed talked about frequency of task, exposure time, number of workers exposed, external influences, fall distance and obstructions that could be hit during a fall. Knowing this information would naturally lead to better, more proactive decisions.

This was such a smart thing to do, but I wasn't sure management would see the value and support it. I decided to contact Colin to see if he had any insight on fall hazard risk assessments. I also wanted to thank him again for his recommendation on trainers.

Colin's company had not conducted a full-scale fall hazard risk assessment. It was probably too much to hope we could just shadow everything his organization did. But, he was having the same experience of heightened awareness and continual identification of new hazards, so his company's management began talking about doing a risk assessment, too. He had received some advice from another colleague who had recently conducted a full site-wide risk assessment. Colin gave me his contact information.

My conversation with Colin's contact, Justin, convinced me more than ever that we needed to do a full-scale risk assessment.

"We conducted our assessment almost a year ago, and we are systematically working through a prioritized list of hazards," Justin said. "Our list is organized by location, maintenance task and type of solution proposed, so we can look at the data through those categories or as a whole. Basically, with our fall hazards and the potential risks associated with them identified, evaluated and ranked, our leadership team used the information to create a budget, schedule and strategy to reduce risk."

"That all sounds like great information to have, but is it too much? Is it overwhelming to get your hands around?" I asked.

Justin laughed.

"That is definitely how we reacted to it at first, since more than 700 hazards were identified during our assessment. Some of them were minor ladder non-compliance issues. There were even some on a ladder we had just installed. Our consultant also uncovered some hidden hazards I don't think we ever would have found. Some of what they found were risks with existing systems we hadn't considered.

"We know we can't address them all right now," Justin added. "In fact, we've only abated 40 hazards this year. The list lets us track our progress and gives us a beginning and end point. We're using the information to report metrics on the amount of risk reduced for our investment."

"I'm glad you mentioned investment," I said. "I won't ask you what you paid for this, but it seems like a large project that's sure to have a hefty price tag. I'm afraid our management might think the cost will outweigh the benefit." I was picturing Derek in my head.

"I don't care what kind of organization you work for," Justin said. "Money is always an issue and our situation was no different. We were able to show how doing the assessment up front could actually save money in the long-term."

Justin was speaking Derek's language, which needed to be my language if I was going to get this approved.

"It's intuitive that better planning upfront allows you to make better decisions, but do you have any good points about costs and benefits I can use to help convince my management team?" I said.

"Our company is very process-oriented, so I knew having a process rather than just devoting resources to today's squeaky wheel would be preferred," Justin said. "By understanding the risk ranking of each hazard, we're able to direct the available budget to the highest risk items, essentially achieving maximum risk reduction for the investment—no matter how big or small our available funds are."

He closed with: "Our financial people liked that explanation, especially when the consultant we used backed it up with real dollars and figures from a previous assessment he had conducted. When they saw how the data could lead us to getting the biggest bang for our buck while reducing our overall risk, they were sold."

It all sounded great to me. Being able to compare risk and cost would satisfy everyone's interests because we would have to look at safety in the context of our budget.

"One other thing," Justin added. "We found it was helpful from both the safety and cost standpoints to have evaluated potential solutions during the risk assessment. That allowed us to consider our options before investing in equipment or design. We've found we're able to select the right systems and address the greatest risks first, so what we did during the risk assessment actually saves us time and money during the hazard control phase."

I thanked Justin for his time and insight. I had to call Colin back, too, and thank him for the referral. I felt smarter about risk assessments, and I was glad to see that Justin's experience backed up what our trainers had told us. A fall hazard risk assessment was the right way to go.

I asked myself, "Now, how to sell it to Derek? If I can sell it to him, I think the rest of the management team would come on board."

## Chapter 6

# Any volunteers? Testing existing systems

It didn't hit me right away when I talked with Justin, but as I reflected on our conversation, I kept going back to his comment about uncovering risks within their existing fall protection systems. What if the systems we had in place — systems our people use all the time — were as risky as the hazards we had not identified?

The guys in our plant certainly don't lack bravado, but I doubt they would have volunteered to take a fall with the fall protection systems we had. I had never considered an evaluation of existing systems as part of a risk assessment, but we needed to do one.

The way I look at it, a fall protection system's sole purpose is to save a falling worker. I didn't have much confidence ours could do that. I decided to go back to Pete to ask him about our systems.

"Well, if it isn't our little Fall Protection Guru," Pete said jokingly as I walked in. "What can I do for you?"

"I'm just here to ask more questions," I said. "This time I want to talk about the systems we have in place. Since we've all admitted we don't, or didn't, know much about fall protection,

I'm curious about whether we should use any of the systems we have in place now."

"I hear what you're asking, but I wouldn't go that far," Pete said. "We had engineers design our systems. We didn't just throw something up there willy-nilly. We have drawings somewhere, I think."

"I guess what I'm really wondering is how can we know for sure the systems are right?" I said. "I don't want to give people a false sense of security — just put on a harness and tie off to this system and everything will be fine. Can we confidently say that and watch our co-workers work at height from these systems?"

I knew I sounded a little dramatic, but I could foresee someone getting hurt by using one of our systems. I wanted to prove to workers the systems were safe.

"Can we ask our own engineers to check the drawings or run some calculations?" I said.

"We could do that, but I'm not sure that would fully accomplish what you want," Pete said. "That's the trouble with fall protection. It's complex because it involves engineering and behavioral safety issues."

"Behavioral safety?" I said. "I remember talking about that in training. I remember the gist of what the trainers said about it. How would you describe it?"

"Well, an engineer can tell you if the anchorage point is strong enough to take the force of a fall," he explained. "But that's not the only thing that matters. You need to know if the training and procedures are correct for the situation and if your equipment is compatible and appropriate. You really need someone who knows both engineering and behavioral safety to evaluate a system."

I understood Pete's explanation, but I suspected finding such a person would be difficult. I couldn't think of anyone I knew who had both skill sets.

"If we had better records, we might be able to do some decent evaluations," Pete said. "But you've seen the state of our records. I doubt we could certify a system with the information we currently have on file."

"Certify?" I asked. "Is that really a thing? What makes a system certified?"

"Honestly, I can't tell you exactly off the top of my head," Pete said. "I know one of the newer ANSI standards gives guidelines for certification."

"Well, Pete, since I took all your standards from you, I guess I better go read them and find out what we need to do," I said. "I'll be back to ask more questions or look for documentation later. Thanks again."

"Anything to help the Fall Protection Guru," he said with a laugh. "But seriously, I support what you're doing, so just let me know what you need."

I kicked myself as I walked back to my desk. There was nothing in the OSHA regulations about certification. I should have known the ANSI standards would have been a good place to start with all my questions. I'm glad Pete knew enough to point me in the right direction. With a little searching, I found information on certification of active fall protection systems in ANSI Z359.6.

I gathered from the standards that certification was important because changes in personnel and work environments can turn a perfectly good system into an unsafe one. That made sense to me, since change happens so quickly anymore. It's smart to check periodically to make sure other changes haven't impacted a system, especially when that change could mean the difference between life and death.

Over the weekend, as I thought about the risk assessment, I wondered which was riskier: the hazards we didn't even know about, or the ones that might exist in the systems our people were using. Should you be more worried about the enemy you know or the one you don't?

I pondered that question when we joined Angela and the kids that Saturday. I tried not to, but I always thought about Steve's accident whenever I was with his family. I was sure someday that would stop, but it was still too fresh, especially while I was knee-deep in the issue.

I could not stop thinking about the fall protection program. I wondered if Steve's tragic death would have been easier or harder to take if a fall protection system had been in place but had not worked. What if Steve would have been tied off to one of our existing systems but fell and died anyway?

Maybe OSHA would be more forgiving if there was at least a system in place. Maybe our staff would feel better knowing that some semblance of safety was provided.

As I watched Angela and the kids play in the fallen leaves, I felt certain it didn't matter much to them. Their loved one was gone either way.

I mentioned my inner dialogue to Cheryl later that night.

"This idea of giving our staff a false sense of security is really eating at me," I said. "I'm not confident in our systems, but I'm not sure it's smart to erode the staff's confidence even further by taking the systems out of use."

"Maybe you're getting ahead of yourself," Cheryl said. "Maybe the systems are OK and you don't have to worry about it. If you can close them down temporarily, I think the employees would appreciate knowing you are proactively checking them to ensure their safety."

"I guess that could work toward more momentum for the fall protection program and overall focus on safety," I said.

"OK, so why don't you seem excited about it?" Cheryl asked. "Checking the systems sounds like another step in the right direction to me."

"It is," I said, still sounding defeated. "The problem is that I wasn't authorized to pursue certification of existing systems. I know Derek will view this as another time and money suck. I don't want the whole thing to get shut down because I keep asking for too much."

Cheryl thought about that for a minute, then lit up with an idea.

"Why don't you ask Derek or key members of his staff to volunteer to take a fall from the systems?" she said. "If they won't do it, why should they be asking their employees to do it?"

Wow, that was bold, I thought. I never pictured Cheryl suggesting something so in-your-face, but she was fired up and invested in what I was doing.

"I don't know," I said. "I feel like that's almost bullying Derek into giving me my way. I'm not sure that's the best approach."

"Well, think about it," Cheryl said. "Maybe the team will hear your logic for wanting to evaluate the systems and give you the go ahead. If you get pushback, you can have this idea in your hip pocket."

I thought about it for the next few days. I talked with Ted and Pete separately and they both agreed with me in principle. We shouldn't give our employees a false sense of security. One way or another, we needed to know if our people were safe using those systems.

I was forced to make a decision by Friday since I was invited into the management team meeting to report on the progress of our fall protection issues. The discussion started with an update on the OSHA investigation into Steve's death. It wasn't pleasant for the company. I was hoping the news about the investigation would get people in the right mindset.

I started with an upbeat report on the success of our first fall protection training session. In addition to the number of people trained, I relayed several anecdotes of changed behavior and evidence of a shift in our safety culture. Derek's expression told me he wasn't impressed. I'm sure he wanted more concrete evidence of success given the time and expense we had devoted so far.

After my report on training, I explained our general program needs, mostly from the information I'd learned from reading the ANSI standards.

"My perception is that we are substantially behind where we need to be in every element of a fall protection program," I said. "Even without being a full-blown expert in this subject, I can tell by researching the standards that we are falling short in most areas."

Derek immediately interrupted me.

"So, you're saying we should be prepared for a slew of OSHA violations?" Derek said. "Are we at significant financial risk?"

I answered as confidently as I could, knowing he might ignore my explanation.

"I can't currently quantify the level of financial risk we may face directly from OSHA," I said. "One thing I do know is that fall fatalities, and even more so with disabling injuries, cost the company a lot of money.

"Honestly, I haven't focused specifically on the OSHA regulations, because they are so complex, yet not specific at the same time," I added. "They're also wildly outdated. I'm confident if we follow the guidelines in the ANSI standards, we will be compliant with OSHA."

Derek quickly countered.

"So, you're telling us we should voluntarily do a bunch of extra stuff OSHA doesn't even require."

As everyone in the room stared at me, I took a moment to calm down before I answered.

"Technically, yes. We cannot give our employees the best safety environment by only doing the bare minimum OSHA requires," I said with as much confidence as I could muster.

At that moment, I realized I was representing the entire workforce as I responded to Derek. They needed an advocate.

"In light of the recent accident," I said as I narrowed my eyes at Derek, "I think our employees need to know we're doing all we can to protect them, not just the minimum legal requirements."

Derek rolled his eyes but said nothing. Thankfully, Ted stepped in and asked me to proceed with my recommendations.

With my confidence bolstered, I got through my overview of the necessary program elements. I mentioned the need for a fall hazard risk assessment to fulfill the hazard identification and evaluation element. Derek perked up from his bored slouch when I started talking about ways to get the most benefit for our investment in fall protection.

I had everyone's attention, so I explained the concept of system certification for our existing systems.

True to form, Derek spoke up and challenged whether this was necessary.

"We already paid to have these systems designed once," he said. "Now, we have to pay someone else to check them? Aren't we going overboard here?"

I explained the value of system certification. I talked about a false sense of security for workers and giving our people a greater confidence in our commitment to protecting them. Derek listened, but I don't think he accepted what I said. He went right back to his original objection.

"OSHA isn't saying we must do this, and we had engineers — professional engineers — design these once. I don't see why we're even talking about this."

That was too flippant for me. As I thought about my response, I looked down at my hip pocket and weighed whether I should follow Cheryl's suggestion and urge Derek to test the systems himself.

Again, Ted bought me some time.

"Derek, are you saying we should just continue using the systems as before? Or, do you have another suggestion?" Ted said.

"We never questioned these systems before. Why are we assuming everything is wrong now?" Derek said.

My emotions got the best of me. I couldn't let that comment go unchallenged.

"Because someone died, Derek. My best friend, Steve, died because we didn't know or didn't care about fall protection."

The room went silent.

"I know Steve's death wasn't from a faulty system," I said. "But everything I've learned from training and research says putting people in fall protection equipment isn't always the answer. In fact, it should be a last resort, and that's even when it's done correctly."

"Knowing what I know now about fall protection," I added, "I don't want to ask any of our people to use those systems until we know for sure they are safe."

I calmed down just enough to proceed without anger in my voice.

"Derek, I am not personally confident in those systems and I would not use them," I said. "If you want to volunteer to fall from each system to prove they're safe, that's the only no-cost alternative I can offer. Of course, it's only no cost if you don't die."

# Chapter 7

# The 20-foot principle

Tension filled the room after that exchange. Ted again stepped in to move the conversation forward.

"Dan, thanks for bringing all these points to our attention. Please appreciate that this is a lot to take in and think about. I suggest we do a few things to better develop our ideas about next steps for fall protection."

The words "next steps for fall protection" encouraged me. That meant there would be next steps, which showed movement in the right direction.

I left the meeting with a few action items, none of which included watching Derek take a fall. But I was making progress. I was to come to the next meeting with information on three things:

The management team wanted to see budget numbers for a site-wide fall hazard risk assessment. That included one number for a basic risk assessment and one that included an existing system evaluation.

Regarding the system certification issue, they asked me to develop a potential compromise to existing system use — something between full use and complete shutdown.

Finally, they asked me to provide a report on the new system at the accident location, basically answering whether this one was done right.

I needed to tap into my resources for help with the first two items. I started by talking with our fall protection consultant, our safety staff and my go-to colleague, Colin.

I was most anxious to talk to Mark about the new system at the site where Steve fell. I had been curious about it, but hadn't asked many questions yet, partly because I didn't want to see the site and partly because I was afraid I would be seen as stepping on Mark's toes.

That evening, when I updated Cheryl about the developments in the meeting, I told her, "I am so glad management gave me permission to ask questions about the new system. I think if I just went poking around on my own, it might upset Mark and others.

"I truly believe Mark is a smart guy and has good intentions to make things right," I said. "But there's no denying we haven't historically been doing the right things. I hope I'll see a great solution, but I'm skeptical."

Cheryl said she understood how I felt and asked great questions to keep me thinking.

"So, how are you going to handle the report?" she said. "Can you submit a negative report without making Mark look bad?"

That would be tricky. But I was getting ahead of myself again, assuming there would be problems with the system. Maybe it was done exactly the way it should have been. I would just have to get in there and find out.

The next week, I met with Mark to review the new system. To his credit, Mark was incredibly open and accepting during the meeting.

I tried to start the conversation on a positive note.

"Mark, I know you were thrown into this task at a difficult time for the company and have had to endure OSHA scrutiny already," I said. "In comparison, talking to me should be a walk in the park. I just need to tell management the system is correct, based on new information we've gathered about fall protection."

"You're right. This wasn't the most coveted assignment in the world," Mark said. "In some ways, I was glad to be a part of this project — to bring something positive to a horrible situation."

He paused and looked at me a little too long for comfort with sympathy in his eyes. He cleared his throat and continued, back in professional mode.

"I feel good about the solution, but I don't know exactly what you need to know for your report," Mark said. "Should I just give you a quick overview?"

Thankfully, Mark was professional and prepared. He walked me through the basics of the solution. It was a personal fall arrest system that required workers to don a full-body harness and attach to an anchorage point at the platform landing before moving to work at the unprotected edges of the platform.

Mark showed me some calculations an engineer had completed for the anchorage point and explained the process for accessing the area and using the system.

As we talked, I remembered something from the fall protection training course we conducted. The trainers mentioned the saying about walking a mile in another's shoes is fitting for many aspects of life, including fall protection.

As the thought came to me, I blurted: "What do the workers think about it?"

Mark was taken aback by the question and said he didn't know. He hadn't asked the workers about their opinions on the solution.

"Do you remember when the trainers told us about the 20-foot principle?" I said.

"That phrase sounds vaguely familiar," Mark said. "Is that the idea that people who work within 20 feet of a problem are most likely to have ideas on how to solve it?"

"That's right," I said. "I think the main idea is that by seeking input, you can make sure you aren't forcing workers to use a system that doesn't fit the tasks they need to perform."

I hesitated a moment.

"Remember the story the fall protection trainers told about the system that was installed before workers were consulted about it? The first time the workers heard about the system was as it was being installed, and there were serious issues. I think the workers even refused to use it. I still remember the way the trainers described the system — technically correct, but functionally impractical."

"I remember the story now that you mention it," Mark said. "I wish I would have thought of it sooner. We didn't work with the staff when we developed this solution. Wasn't that the point the trainers made — getting their input before a solution is implemented? I guess we missed the boat."

"Maybe," I said. "I'd still like to know what they think at this point."

"Honestly, I haven't heard any feedback either way," Mark said. "It's only been in use a few days though. Do you think there's still value in asking, or do you think they're just going to accept what has been installed and move on?"

That was hard to say, but I still wanted to try.

"You may have gotten better buy-in or new ideas about the system upfront by talking with the employees, but I still think it's good to ask their opinion now, especially since they've used the system and can give specific examples from their experience."

"I agree that it's good to ask the staff for feedback," Mark said "If nothing else, it shows we care about their opinions. It could be good for morale in that way, but I'd be surprised if they know enough to develop a new solution."

I quickly countered.

"We don't necessarily need the employees to develop a solution, or in this case, a new solution," I said. "It's just good to get their insight about the tasks since they're the ones actually facing the hazard. The safety staff can work through the specifics to come up with a functional solution that is compliant."

Mark and I brainstormed for a few minutes about who to talk with and what questions to ask. He was more concerned with the technical aspects of the system, talking about aspects like anchorage strength and equipment components. I wanted to know the practicality of them.

I had a lot of questions. I wanted to know if workers fully understood how to use the system. It's one thing to provide a system, but it's pretty useless if they don't feel properly trained, or even properly protected by it.

I was curious about what they would change about the solution if they were in charge. And, from a practical standpoint, I wanted to know if they could get to everything they needed to reach, or if they felt limited by it.

I wouldn't ask it, but the biggest question for me was still whether this system would have saved Steve's life.

## Chapter 8

# Do you want a harness with that?

After Mark and I worked out the details of our employee interviews about the new fall protection system, I took the conversation back to the beginning. I wanted to understand how we got to this point.

"How did you decide on a personal fall arrest system as the solution?" I said.

Mark looked at me with confusion, despite what I considered to be a simple question.

"Well, management asked me to install a solution to protect workers, and this just seemed like an obvious answer," Mark said.

"I had just talked to our fall protection equipment rep a few weeks before, so I called him for help," Mark added. "He knows our equipment better than we do, and I assumed he could figure out if we could use the harnesses and lanyards we already have on site. Derek was adamant we keep the solution cost low, so I thought reusing existing equipment would be best."

Mark's answer took me back to the initial Internet research I did when I started looking at fall protection. I was overwhelmed by the amount of available equipment, to the point where I struggled to find information about anything other than equipment.

"OK, so you and the equipment rep determined this system was the most appropriate solution?" I clarified.

"Yes, when I explained the situation and showed him the area, he suggested this type of system," Mark said. "I was already thinking something similar, so we moved forward."

"Did you guys discuss any other alternatives?" I said, trying not to sound critical. "Did you think about using a lift, or installing guardrail or anything like that?"

"Not really," Mark said. "We knew the fall arrest system would work in this space and we already had some equipment we could reuse."

I had to ask these questions because it seemed like it would be much safer and productive for the workers if guardrail had been installed — a passive control (as our trainers called it), something that was there waiting to protect workers rather than equipment they had to inspect and put on each time they needed it.

Of course it didn't surprise me that Derek had suggested something simple and cheap rather than the best solution for the safety of the employees. I knew he wasn't totally cold-hearted, but it sure seemed like he cared more about money than people.

While these thoughts ran through my head, I realized Mark was still standing there, trying to figure out if we were done with the conversation.

"So, you met with the equipment rep and determined this fall arrest solution was best. Then what?"

"Yes, we decided on this solution," Mark said. "The equipment guys designated an anchor point for the system and brought in some new equipment we needed for it. Our rep showed me and a few other guys how to use it the day they brought the new lanyards in. All the equipment we need is stored in the cabinet over there."

That scenario sounded familiar to me since I had been one of the "other guys" trained on a similar system in another area of the plant a few years ago. This seemed like our standard mode of operation: find a safety hazard, get some equipment, train a few people and move on.

I asked myself: is that wrong? It doesn't seem well thought out or thorough, but some level of protection is being provided.

Since I had developed a greater appreciation for how complex fall protection is, this "throw equipment at it" attitude seemed wrong now.

Until we got more information from the employee interviews, I figured there was nothing more for us to discuss, so we wrapped up the meeting.

As I went about my day job for the rest of the day, I questioned how this solution — and probably dozens of others — was selected.

I remembered how much our trainers had focused on the Hierarchy of Control, which essentially ranks solutions based on effectiveness and "defeatability." Ideally, you want a solution that is as effective as possible and least likely to be defeated by a person's actions.

I distinctly remembered the trainers stressing that equipment-based solutions are at the lowest level on the Hierarchy of Control. They said PPE (Personal Protective Equipment) systems are only as strong as their weakest link. I remembered the image of the broken link in a chain. It was powerful because it was easy to picture someone falling as the link broke.

For this situation, though, it seemed like other options were ignored. The fall arrest gear was considered easy and cheap, so we plowed forward. I felt this was a cavalier attitude since these systems could put people's lives at risk if not done correctly.

I wanted to talk to someone about it, so I caught up with my buddy Pete to get his take on the situation.

Again, I didn't want to be overly critical of how things were done in the past, but I needed to understand where this equipment-first mindset came from.

"Hey, Pete," I said. "It's your resident Fall Protection Guru back with more questions."

Pete laughed and beckoned me into his office. "Anything for you, of course. Come on in."

I told Pete about my conversation with Mark.

"Does it surprise you no one challenged the idea of using a fall arrest system, or at least challenged that we didn't have multiple options to choose from?" I said.

"No, it doesn't surprise me," Pete said. "People around here typically think of equipment when they think of fall protection. They think as long as they're tied off to something, they're protected. Honestly, even I tend to think PPE first and I know better."

"I guess I can't blame you," I said. "Before I started doing all this research and went through good training, the first thing I thought of when someone said fall protection was a harness."

"And I understand your comment about being tied off," I said. "I never really thought about it directly, but I'm sure I felt I was protected if I was tied off. I figured it had been someone's job to make sure everything was right, so I didn't think much about it. That thought is scary to me now that I know how much has to go right for a fall protection system to work properly."

"It's a common trap," Pete said. "When guys need to get the work done, and their supervisor hands them some equipment, they typically just do what they're told and move forward. It's hard because sometimes the solution is spot on."

"True, I guess it is hard for people who aren't properly trained to question the solution," I said. "I think that's what frustrates me about our equipment rep. He didn't even consider or suggest a more passive solution, like a lift or guardrail. Mark came to him for help, and I feel like he wasn't very helpful."

Pete looked at me quizzically.

"What did you expect?" he said. "He's an equipment rep. He knows the most about equipment, and his job is to sell equipment. It's not unsafe or inappropriate, so why wouldn't he suggest a PPE solution if it works? We needed a solution, and the system technically meets the regulations and functions properly."

"I guess," I said. "I think I'm just overly sensitive about it because a passive solution seems obviously better to me. Why am I the only one thinking about that?"

"The market is full of equipment and it's the most visible part of fall protection," Pete said. "Heck, you and I both admitted we tend to think of PPE first. It's sort of the nature of the industry."

"Yeah, that's obvious from the research I've done and from this experience," I said. "It's just that PPE systems have so many opportunities to fail. Even a well-designed system can fail if the anchorage isn't strong enough, a component is incompatible, a procedure isn't followed or workers aren't properly trained."

"That's all true, but there are good things about PPE systems, and the equipment vendors are also readily available," Pete said. "In my experience, it tends to be the easiest and cheapest way to go most of the time."

"Uh-oh," I said. "Have you been talking to Derek too much? I thought he was the easy and cheap solution guy."

Pete laughed.

"Believe me, Derek isn't the only person who tends to go for easy and cheap, especially if it works."

I nodded and said, "Now, the question is: what does it mean to say it works?"

## Chapter 9

# All clear?

After several weeks of coordinating, Mark and I prepared to interview employees who used the new fall protection system at the accident location.

On the morning of the interviews, my wife could tell something was different about me.

"Big day at work today?" she said.

"I don't know," I said. "Probably not. We're interviewing some of the people who are using the new system at the site of Steve's accident. For some reason, I'm really anxious about it — a mix of excitement and nervousness."

"So, what's going to come out of these interviews?" she asked. "Are you more worried about the process or the results?"

I thought about it for a minute.

"The results, I guess," I said. "I want to hear what our people have to say. I'm just not sure anything they say will have an impact on management. Even if this system stays the same, I'm hoping we learn some things to help in the future."

"You never know," Cheryl said. "Somebody may share some great insight that will lead to positive changes. Here's hoping," she said with her characteristic smile and a clink of our orange juice glasses.

The interviews generated a variety of responses, as I knew they would. Some people felt comfortable with the system, the training and the productivity they could achieve. Others were more critical, complaining about everything from lack of detailed training and procedures to the type of harness they had to wear. It was difficult to tell whether the disparity in answers had more to do with the unique experiences or the personalities of the individuals.

Then, during the last interview of the day, an older worker who had only been with LMK about a year, brought up an issue no one else did.

"I feel like I understand the system in general," he said, and then seemed to catch himself from saying more.

"I feel like there was about to be more to that statement," I said, testing to see if I could get him to continue.

"I guess I gave myself away," he said with a slight smile. "Okay, I'm not convinced there is enough fall clearance."

"Fall clearance?" I said. I remembered doing fall clearance calculations during our training course, but I hadn't given it a thought when we first reviewed the system.

"Yeah," he said. "If I'm connected and go over that edge, I'm afraid I would hit that piece of equipment below the platform."

He pointed to a large machine under part of the platform. "See what I mean?" he asked.

I looked at Mark but he said nothing. Instead, he flipped through his notes about the system, presumably looking for something that would show the clearance was adequate.

When Mark remained quiet, I asked the worker to elaborate. I had a general understanding of how to calculate fall clearance, but I wanted to hear more from him.

"Well, I haven't actually done any calculations," he said. "But based on what I remember about clearances, it seems to me there is no way the system would stop a fall before I hit that machine. It's only, what, 6 feet from the platform?"

I looked at the layout, and he was close with a guess of 6 feet. I saw his point, but I wanted him to keep talking.

"You're probably right," I said. "I'm pretty new to fall protection. Could you explain more about why that distance is a problem?"

"The lanyard on the system is a 6-footer, and the anchor point is at ground level," he said.

"OK, I see," I said. "Keep going."

"So," he said, "it's a few feet from the anchor point to where the lanyard is attached to my back. Once the lanyard is stretched, you get the 6 feet of lanyard to arrest the fall. By that time, it seems like you would have already hit the machine below."

60

His explanation made sense, but we needed to do some specific calculations to see if his assumptions were correct. If he was right, my worst fears would be confirmed: we've been asking people to attach to a system that won't necessarily protect them.

While we talked, Mark was busy taking notes and flipping through the information he had on the system design. Mark and I needed to talk about this.

"Thanks so much for your willingness to bring up this issue," I told the worker. "Please know we're going to perform formal calculations to confirm if there is a clearance issue."

I wanted to tell him not to use the system until we looked into the issue further, but I didn't have the authority to do that. Thankfully, Mark was concerned and did have the authority.

"I am taking this system out of service today," Mark said. "I will be in touch with your supervisor and the rest of your team about this. I don't want anyone using this until we look into the clearance issue."

"Is that necessary?" the worker asked, which took me aback. I couldn't imagine why he would question the need to make sure the system was safe.

"I've had this concern since the system was installed, but I've just been extra careful, especially when I'm over the portion above that machine," the worker said. "I've told the other guys the same, so we should be OK using it while you investigate."

As he talked, I suspected he had some fears about being a whistleblower. I told him, "I appreciate you sharing your concerns with us, and with the other members of your team. Is there any reason why you haven't come forward to your supervisor or management about this?"

"Well," he said timidly, "I wasn't totally sure I was right. Plus, I knew everyone was anxious to get a system in place. I didn't want to be the guy that halted progress. I figured giving people a little warning would be enough."

I thought about Steve's accident. Had he thought about being careful when he went to loosen that bolt? Did he realize he was in a precarious position? Did he give his own safety a thought, or was he just focused on getting the job done?

I assured the worker he wouldn't get in any trouble for bringing the issue forward.

"I understand your concern about halting progress, but the safety of our employees has to be our top priority," I said. "We will investigate your concerns, and your name and interview will not be mentioned.

"You know, you may have saved someone's life today by bringing this information forward," I said. "Thank you on behalf of the entire company."

With that, we ended the interview and Mark and I set off to debrief each other on what we had learned from the staff.

My first question to Mark was: "Is he right? Do we have a clearance problem?"

"I don't know," Mark said "His explanation of the flaws in the system made sense, but I don't have any calculations to prove it one way or the other. I would have thought we would have some documentation, but I'm not seeing anything in the paperwork from the designer."

"Well, we clearly need to do those calculations today," I said. "You promised to take the system out of service, so I think that needs to be the first order of business. I suggest you take care of that and I'll get my clearance calculation notes from training. Let's meet back at the system after lunch."

While Mark took care of the system shutdown, I reviewed my training manual and some online tools related to fall clearance. I refreshed my memory on the variables included in the clearance calculation: free fall, deceleration distance, stretch out and a safety margin. I remembered thinking it was complicated, but the information was readily available. I felt comfortable Mark and I could have an answer by day's end.

As I ate lunch at my desk, Ted and Derek approached. Ted looked purposeful and Derek looked like his usual agitated self.

Ted started to talk, but Derek quickly cut him off.

"So, what's this we hear about shutting the system down?" Derek barked. "Are you trying to scare people?"

His demeanor infuriated me, but I was confident the right steps had been taken. I had no problem answering Derek's assault.

"You're right. Mark and I decided to shut the system down temporarily to determine if we have a fall clearance issue. That is the feedback we received from the staff interviews, so it needs to be checked before we ask employees to use the system."

"So, that whole area is just shut down?" Derek railed. "Is that what you're telling me?"

"Not exactly," I said calmly. "Just no work from that particular platform until we have an answer on the clearance issue. Mark and I are meeting in an hour and should have an answer today."

Ted interjected. "So, we'll be back to full capacity by the end of the day?" Ted asked.

"Maybe," I said. "If our calculations show the system doesn't provide enough fall clearance, we'll have to keep the system shut down until corrections can be made or another solution can be put in place."

Derek didn't like that uncertainty.

"How long will that be?" he said. "Isn't there an alternative to shutting everything down indefinitely?"

Ted stepped in again.

"Can you explain what the issue is, and what you and Mark are doing about it? We don't fully understand the severity of the issue," Ted said, emphasizing the "we" and shooting a look at Derek.

I gave them the quick and dirty version of the story.

"The way the system was designed and installed, we believe it's possible for a worker to use the system properly and still hit something below the platform if they fall. Mark and I will perform the necessary calculations to confirm whether this is, in fact, a problem with the system."

"So, you're saying even if workers do exactly what they're supposed to, a fall could still result in an injury?" Ted said.

"Yes, exactly," I said. "It seems this aspect of the system design was overlooked. We need to know exactly what we're facing before we ask workers to use the system again."

"I'm sure it's fine," Derek said. "We had this thing professionally designed."

"True," I said. "This is a unique and complex aspect of fall protection. If we used a structural engineer who doesn't know much about fall protection, the clearance issue can be easily overlooked."

I continued, feeling like I was channeling our fall protection trainers.

"Clearance isn't about strength of the anchorage or the system," I said. "Even if everything else about the system is perfect, not having enough clearance means a person hits the ground or something else before the system even has a chance to work. That's what we're trying to avoid."

Ted appeared to understand and Derek didn't have much left to say.

"I want to know what you find out … TODAY," Derek said, storming off muttering something about productivity.

As we both watched him go, Ted closed the conversation.

"I think you and Mark are doing the right thing, but we need to be sensitive about what this does to production, operations, employee morale — all of it," Ted said. "In his own strange way, Derek is looking out for the company, trying to make sure we aren't making unnecessary sacrifices."

"I understand, and we will get you an answer today," I said. "Derek left before I could make the point he needs to hear, one that he would pay attention to."

"Should I get him back over here?" Ted said.

"No. I can bring this up with him later if necessary," I said. "He needs to understand that even if the clearance distance we are lacking is only a little bit short, a worker could strike the equipment below, maybe even just his lower half. Obviously, injured is better than dead. But from a financial perspective, it actually costs the company more if someone has a disabling injury. From both the personal and financial risk standpoints, we have to care about this."

"Well, that's a little sick to think about, but I'm sure you're right," Ted said. "You can bring this up with the larger group at some point, so the entire team understands the financial risk we could face. Let's leave Derek alone for now."

As Ted turned to leave, I added a plug for our risk assessment project.

"Ted, this is why I felt so strongly about including existing systems in a potential risk assessment project. Clearly, our systems aren't perfect and we may be endangering our people."

"One thing at a time, Dan," he said. "Let's figure out what to do about this system and then we'll tackle the risk assessment. I don't think Derek can handle much more right now," he said with a smirk as he walked out the door.

Before my meeting with Mark, I asked myself whether it would be better to get a result of adequate clearance or not enough. If it was adequate, management would settle down, we would go back into full production, and the workers would have more assurance the system would protect them. Hopefully, they would feel good we had confirmed the system's safety and their feedback was important.

On the other hand, if the clearance distance wasn't adequate, it would justify changes to how we operate. We could get more employee feedback and have better leverage for investigating other systems around the plant. I know more investigation would make me feel better, but it may be hard to rationalize if this system was fine.

I met with Mark to perform the calculation. We decided to each perform the clearance calculation independently to see if we arrived at the same answer.

As it turned out, the machine in question was 6.5 feet below the platform. Mark and I both came to same conclusion about the necessary clearance. We needed more than double the amount of clearance to fully arrest a fall without striking the machine below.

"Wow," Mark said as we realized what we had discovered. "That's a little scary. We could have had another injury or death on our hands."

"At least we know we have a problem and can fix it. Now, which one of us gets to break the news to Derek?" I said, only half-joking. "This isn't going to be welcome news, but we have the numbers to back up our conclusion."

After toying with the idea of flipping for it, we decided we needed to present a unified front to management. We called Derek and Ted together and shared the news.

Derek was visibly annoyed, but he knew he couldn't ignore the issue. Ted listened to our explanation and said to Mark, "Get it fixed as soon as possible. The system will stay shut down until it's right."

Mark and I walked away discussing our next steps.

"I guess you were right. We probably should have looked at guardrail or something else," Mark said. "Having to rework this system is going to be a hassle, and I don't know how quickly we can get an answer and make the modifications."

"Herein lies the problem with these PPE-based systems," I said. "There are too many ways to screw it up."

"As they say, admitting you have a problem is half the battle," Mark said. "I think it's safe to say we have a problem."

# Chapter 10

# Rescue me. Please.

As Mark worked on fixing the existing system, I used my fall protection time to work on the other two items I needed to give management: a budget for a risk assessment and a recommendation about how to handle our existing systems.

Now that I had seen the flaws with the new system, I did not want to compromise on how to proceed with our other existing systems. I wanted to ask management for a shutdown of all existing systems as well as a full risk assessment that included existing systems. But I had a feeling that might be too much, especially if I didn't provide an alternative.

I spent some more time with our fall protection consultant, our safety staff and my buddy, Colin, to get some additional perspective on these issues.

I asked our fall protection consultant and another firm Colin recommended to provide proposals for the risk assessment project, with and without an existing system evaluation. I also asked them to provide a scope and price for conducting a "pilot" assessment where only a portion of the plant would be assessed. I thought a smaller area and price may be more palatable to management, but would still show real results.

I told Ted about my ideas on the risk assessment and he liked the different options management would have to consider. He agreed that providing options would be the best tactic.

"To be honest, Ted, I'm struggling a little bit more with recommendations related to our existing systems," I said. "I talked to a few colleagues at other organizations and I wasn't crazy about any of their suggestions, either.

"I feel like we're in a tough place," I said. "Anything less than taking the systems out of commission seems irresponsible, since we — or at least, I — don't have much confidence in them. But I realize taking every system out of service could have a major impact on our ability to execute. Some of my colleagues suggested adding restrictive signage or requiring a safety department check before each use of a system. Those just seem like Band-Aids over the issues."

"I understand how you feel," Ted said. "Hearing we had problems with a new system was very concerning to me, but maybe a Band-Aid is the best we can do until we have a better handle on what our issues really are. I would rather try something like that than do nothing at all."

It wasn't what I wanted to hear, but Ted was trying to be practical.

"So, do you think a full investigation into our existing system is out of the question?" I said.

"Not necessarily," Ted said. "But I don't think the fact one system had a flaw is enough to convince the team to take on such a large-scale evaluation of our systems, especially if they're also being asked to consider the general risk assessment project. I think it's all too new and unknown, and probably too expensive."

"OK. I see what you mean," I said. "What do you think about applying the pilot concept to the system evaluation issue? I mean, what if we select a subset of systems — maybe the most frequently used or the oldest — and have a fall protection expert evaluate them. Maybe limit it to a half a dozen so it's manageable, but shows if we have a trend of inadequate systems?"

Ted said that idea had a better chance of acceptance than a full shutdown and evaluation of all systems. He gave me approval to proceed. He also gave me an extension for reporting to the management team. This pilot evaluation would take some time.

"Don't forget," Ted said. "We still need a temporary solution for how to instruct our employees about system use in the interim. You still might have to bring in a Band-Aid."

I thanked Ted for the advice and the permission to proceed with more evaluations. I immediately contacted our fall protection consultant to see how quickly he could evaluate the systems and collaborated with Pete and Mark to pick out six systems for evaluation.

A few weeks later, our consultant was on site for a couple of days, working through the evaluation of the six systems we selected. As much as my schedule allowed, I followed him around, learning about the different aspects he evaluated and asking other questions that had been on my mind.

When our consultant presented the evaluation report to me, the results confirmed what I had suspected. All but one system had significant issues. Some had the same fall clearance issue as our new system, others had incompatible or damaged equipment components, and they all lacked written procedures for use.

As we discussed the results of the evaluations, our consultant focused on the need for use and rescue procedures.

"Not one of your systems has a documented procedure for use or rescue," the consultant said. "It can be dangerous to trust that word-of-mouth instructions are enough to properly use a system. It can be deadly to have no plan for rescuing a fallen worker."

"To be honest," I said, "I don't know exactly how people are supposed to know how to use a system or rescue someone around here. I guess I assumed the right people were trained on the right things when a system was installed. I have no idea what the rescue plan is for the systems I was trained to use."

"That's probably because you don't have a rescue plan," he said. "In our work, we have found rescue is one of the most overlooked aspects of fall protection. A lot of time, people assume they'll just call 9-1-1 or figure it out in the moment. Or, just as often, they don't think about rescue at all until someone is hanging there suspended and no one knows what to do."

He explained the importance of rescue.

"Imagine the relief a fallen worker feels when they realize a fall arrest system has worked — that they were just saved from a life-threatening plummet," he said.

I pictured myself falling and being saved. I smiled and felt the sense of relief he described.

"Now imagine the panic that sets in when the worker realizes there is no rescue plan in place — that no one knows what to do, what equipment to use or who to call."

I didn't like imagining that part at all.

"When a system is put in place properly, a rescue plan is already determined," he said. "Some rescue scenarios can be complicated, but many times an effective rescue can be accomplished by simply using a portable ladder. The simplest plan is often the best. It just needs to be thought through in advance so the right people and equipment are ready when needed."

"Having heard that, I'm not surprised we don't have adequate rescue plans," I said. "I can't remember us ever talking about this issue before."

"It's not surprising," he said. "Even the most proactive companies tend to minimize or ignore the need for fall protection rescue.

"Here's an example: one organization's rescue plan called for fallen workers to reach their mobile phones and call 9-1-1 themselves. They didn't consider the fact that a medical emergency, trauma during the fall, or simply a circumstance where a worker couldn't reach their phone would render this plan ineffective."

I pictured someone hanging in a harness trying desperately to get to the phone in their pants pocket. Slim chance.

"We always caution people against relying solely or blindly on calling 9-1-1," he said. "Depending on the circumstances and capabilities of your local rescue services, they may not get a fallen worker down in time to prevent serious injury or death. You better know that before you have someone hanging, counting on you to save their life."

I never thought of rescue as part of the life-saving process of fall protection.

"Is hanging in a harness really life threatening?" I said. "I had never thought about that before."

"It absolutely can be life threatening," he said. "There have been many scientific studies about this, and there is no set amount of time when medical issues begin to occur, since every person is different."

"Have you ever suspended in a harness before?" he asked me. "How long would you want to stay suspended?"

"The only time I've ever suspended is part of an equipment demo years ago and during training with you guys a few months ago," I said. "Each time, I was probably suspended less than a minute, and I was certainly ready to get down."

"I know how you feel," he said. "It's not the most pleasant feeling in the world, but rescuing someone in one minute is pretty unrealistic."

"So, what should a rescue plan shoot for in terms of time?" I said.

"The regulations aren't terribly clear on that issue," he said. "An OSHA bulletin recommends getting someone to the ground within 30 minutes. The ANSI standards we discussed during training require you to make at least verbal contact with a fallen worker within six minutes."

"As usual, the ANSI standards are a bit more rigorous and specific," I said.

"Yes," he said. "The ANSI standards include an entire document just on rescue and rescue equipment, as well as additional guidance on rescue in the program standard.

"The moral of the story is you don't want to get caught halfway protecting your workers," he said. "If you spend the time, money and resources to protect people from going through a fall, you can't leave out the next steps to ensure their safety. Rescue isn't an afterthought or a good idea. It has to be an essential part of the planning and execution of your fall protection systems."

I got great information from our consultant. He even sent me some of the research studies about the topic of suspension trauma — what happens to someone who hangs in a harness too long. It was fascinating stuff, although I still couldn't imagine hanging for 40-plus minutes as some of the test subjects had done. No way!

The information the consultant provided about the lack of use and rescue procedures — in addition to the other deficiencies they found — justified a closer look at more of our existing systems.

With the data from our pilot evaluations, I could show the lives of our workers were being threatened each time we asked them to use our systems.

When I presented the evaluation results to the management team, I got the usual divided response. Some people understood the severity of our deficiencies and wanted to move forward with a phased approach to correcting the systems. Others were less supportive.

"I see the need to make a few adjustments, but isn't it a little dramatic to say we're putting people's lives at risk just because we haven't written down how to rescue them?" Derek said.

"I wouldn't call it dramatic," I said. "We have fall clearance issues, equipment issues and an overriding lack of use and rescue procedures. There are many problems, any one of which could cause another incident if we don't make changes. No one predicted Steve's accident would happen, and we can't predict where the next one will be, either."

I didn't like the way Derek belittled the rescue issue.

"The lack of rescue planning is a serious issue," I said. "The data on suspension trauma is scary, and I know from experience how unpleasant being suspended is. We can't just hope our people figure out what to do when the time comes."

I added another point I thought would shut Derek down.

"Plus, if an OSHA compliance officer sequences the events after an incident and determines we were negligent in planning or action, we can face citations and penalties. There is a precedent for citations based on inappropriate or ineffective rescue plans.

"The point is we have documented deficiencies with many of our systems," I said. "If we're going to correct those deficiencies, we need to include rescue plans with the new designs or procedures. That part isn't necessarily going to be complicated or expensive. It just has to be done."

I pushed Derek on the severity of our issues.

"My offer still stands, Derek," I said. "If you want to take a fall from each system to test it, we can still go that route. We can just let people figure out in the moment how to rescue you from each one. Is that how you want to create our rescue plans?"

Derek clearly didn't appreciate the challenge, but he needed to stop being so flippant about what we were asking workers to do.

"Dan, be serious. You know I'm not going to do that. I realize you view me as the bad guy here, but we don't have unlimited time and resources to create a perfect program. Somebody has to be practical here."

We didn't make any final decisions that day, but the meeting ended on a positive note. The team agreed to consider the risk assessment proposals as part of next year's safety budget. They also asked me to work with Pete to develop a priority order for assessing existing systems and a phasing plan.

I welcomed working with Pete to develop a plan for addressing our systems even if it didn't happen as quickly as I would like. I wanted to involve others, too, so I asked, "Is there any reason not to involve Mark and others in the safety group with the prioritization of systems? I think others may have insights Pete and I don't have."

"Oh, I guess you haven't heard," Ted said. "Mark has submitted his two weeks' notice and is moving on to another company. You better pick his brain about the systems while you can."

I had not heard Mark was leaving LMK. I was disappointed because I considered Mark my fall protection ally.

Ted pulled me aside as the meeting ended.

"Good work," he said. "I think doing the pilot evaluations was the right first step, and the folks around the table are really starting to feel the weight of the risk we're facing. But you can stop suggesting Derek fall from these systems. After what you've shared with us, I wouldn't let anyone fall from these systems."

It was official. Ted was converted and the rest of the management was inching that way.

# Chapter 11

# The fall hazard that wasn't

I felt great about the feedback the management team gave me and wanted to prioritize existing systems immediately. Plus, I wanted to get Mark's thoughts before he left the company.

When I approached Pete and Mark about it on Monday, both said they would help. Mark said he was grateful he could contribute to this important step even as he was on his way out. Since my time was limited, Pete took the lead on creating an updated log of every system in the company. Together, we created a prioritized list and divided it into phases for evaluation and correction.

"I can't thank you guys enough for your help with this," I told Pete and Mark as we completed the list. "I definitely didn't have the background to do this myself. Besides correcting the deficiencies with our systems, I'm really hoping we learn some things so we don't repeat mistakes."

"Well, I've already learned to think about other solutions before equipment-based systems," Mark said. "That came through loud and clear on the new system."

"I have also learned a lot from our consultant," I said. "We know we must have detailed training, instructions and rescue plans for each active system."

"I feel some sort of checklist coming on," Pete joked. "Actually, we do need to capture some sort of best practices or requirements before we ask a designer to provide a system. I think that would really help us make sure everything has been considered upfront."

"Speaking of upfront," Pete said, "I've been reading and hearing a lot about a concept called Prevention through Design. I think it makes really good sense and would appeal to the management team."

"Prevention through Design? I've never heard of it, but if you think the management team would like it, I'm all ears," I said. "What is it?"

"In my layman's terms, it's basically looking at building or process designs and trying to get rid of safety hazards before anything is even built." Pete said.

"That makes good sense," I said. "I assume we're not doing that now?"

"No, not really," Pete said. "Safety folks don't usually get involved until after everything is done and they figure out some part of their work needs protection. That's when we get called in."

We decided to check the Internet for more information before we went any further. The strongest definition we found described it as addressing occupational safety and health needs in the design process to prevent or minimize the work-related hazards and risks associated with the construction,

81

manufacture, use, maintenance, and disposal of facilities, materials and equipment.

Mark said, "I like Pete's simple definition better, but the overall concept to talk about safety during programming and design is really smart."

We all agreed, especially when we found examples that showed how incorporating safety early saves money because designers don't even need to erase lines on their drawings. The safety aspects are simply programmed into the design. The cost factor would be a great selling point to management, and it resulted in greater levels of safety, too — a win-win.

"What it sounds like to me is when safety folks are brought in at the beginning of a project, safety issues can be addressed right away as part of the core project, not after the fact when we have to make it a new project and there are more restrictions," Pete said.

Mark added another point.

"Plus, it seems like understanding the safety issues upfront will increase safety for all workers, from construction guys into operations, and all the way through to routine or emergency maintenance," Mark said.

"I really like this idea," I said. "I don't see how improving safety and saving money at the same time could possibly be bad. Pete, we need to think about this and how we can use this concept to make sure we don't have unsafe systems. Maybe this concept can help us get rid of hazards altogether."

"I think getting rid of hazards altogether is a little far-fetched," Pete said. "But it's definitely a concept worth considering. Are you ready to throw another new concept at the management team? I thought you might want a year or two off from that, you know, to recover."

"You're right," I said with a laugh. "Maybe it's a little too soon. But I'm going to start researching this idea. I think it has legs."

The more I looked into the Prevention through Design concept, the more convinced I became we needed to implement a program for this. Plus, I thought this might be the ticket to getting Derek on board with a fall protection idea. I figured he would love the idea of minimizing fall protection issues altogether and saving money when they had to be addressed. That's basically what he'd been asking for all along. I think he just wanted fall protection to go away, and a Prevention through Design program might be the best way to achieve that—or at least get closer to that.

I continued to research the issue. I read several case studies on the Internet. I also wanted to talk to someone firsthand about it. I decided to reach out to Colin again to see if his company used Prevention through Design.

Colin said his company didn't have a formal Prevention through Design program, but he knew about it and the basic benefits of it.

"For someone in my position, Prevention through Design seems like a no-brainer: reduced safety risk and cost. Why wouldn't we want to do that?"

"That's exactly what I thought when I first learned about this," I said.

"But creating an entire new program changes the way projects are managed," Colin said. "It changes who is involved, when and how. Change isn't always easy, as I'm sure you know.

"So, we don't have a formal program, but we've still seen the general concept work for us," he said. "I'm hoping we can get some momentum for a more formalized Prevention through Design method with some small victories. Remember the elevator example I gave you, where we changed the design at a worker's suggestion to get rid of the need for fall protection?"

"Yes," I said. "You guys were able to eliminate the need for fall protection completely — just change the location of the fan and the fall protection issue goes away."

"Exactly," Colin said. "The guy who pointed out the issue was not a safety professional. He's a maintenance supervisor we put through competent person training last year. Thankfully, he was on the design team and knew enough about fall protection to suggest the change."

"So, that's what you meant about not having a formal program?" I said. "He was knowledgeable and suggested an alternative, but he wasn't on the design team because of his knowledge of safety or fall protection."

"Correct," Colin said. "Of course, in an ideal world, we would always have someone on the design team looking out for safety issues."

My conversation with Colin convinced me even more LMK needed a Prevention through Design program. Even though I concentrated on eliminating fall hazards, a PTD program could eliminate or minimize all types of safety risks. I knew a PTD program would produce great results.

As usual, the difficult part would be convincing management about the value of a program like this, that it was worth the effort to provide training and work through the inherent growing pains of something new.

I decided to start the conversation with Derek. I figured if I could get him on board, the rest of the management team would be a piece of cake.

I'm not Derek's favorite person, so I knew I would have to catch his attention quickly before he put up his defenses. I decided to catch him in a free moment rather than schedule a meeting with him. I didn't want to give him any time to start planning a counter-argument.

As I thought through how to approach Derek, I decided it was best to lead with a compelling example, so I researched some case studies and found a great one. Armed with some key message points and my case study, I knocked on Derek's open door.

"Can I have a few minutes of your time?" I asked. He hesitated, then waved me in.

"I found a dramatic way to save money on fall protection," I said. "I wanted you to be the first to know about it. Plus, with your role in operations, you are the perfect person to help implement it."

Before he could interject, I shared the cost saving results of the case study.

"With this method, the company eliminated costs for design, fabrication and installation, equipment purchases and related training, as well as the risk that comes with working at heights. On another project, they reduced equipment and labor by a factor of six."

"That all sounds great," Derek said. "Is there a catch? Why aren't we already doing things this way if it saves money?" he said. Great question, I thought.

He gave me the opening, so I explained the PTD concept to him as well as some of the things that would need to change to make a PTD program work at our company. To illustrate the concept, I showed him some sample process and program graphics I had found online. I also walked through a few more case studies where other organizations had eliminated hazards or at least programmed safer protection options into original designs.

I could feel myself going on and on, not wanting to leave any message point unsaid or any example unnoticed. Finally, Derek held up his hand to stop me.

"Dan, I realize what you're doing," he said. It was my turn to put up my defenses. To my surprise, Derek continued in a pleasant tone.

"I realize you're putting the full court press on me because I have challenged you at every step of this fall protection journey we've been on," he said. "I can't promise I'll stop doing that. It's sort of my nature to question things and make sure we're being operationally and fiscally responsible."

"Great," I thought. "I can't wait." But, then Derek surprised me, right when I was ready to start defending my position again.

"I have to admit I've seen some really positive cultural changes in the past few months," he said. "I'm still going to be a numbers and process guy, but I can't deny that the changes we've made to our safety program are good for the company in many ways."

This was the first positive comment I had heard from Derek in, well, our entire working relationship. He was still giving himself permission to question, but at least he wasn't immediately dismissive of the PTD idea.

"I'm glad you're seeing the same positive momentum I am," I said. "I really think a PTD program would solidify our commitment to a safe work environment and could truly make good business sense for the process-and-numbers guys."

"Well, I don't know any more about this PTD concept than what you just told me, but I'm willing to at least explore it with you," Derek said.

Those last words really took me by surprise. He was volunteering to work with me on it. I had to ask myself if that was good or bad. I decided it was good even if Derek was only getting involved to make sure I was right. A "yes" is a "yes," so I at least had an opportunity to prove this out.

Derek and I discussed the idea of doing a few pilot projects with this concept before we created and implemented a new program for design and construction projects. The pilot concept made him more comfortable and I was happy to get the chance to produce our own positive results with the program. I knew that would always be more convincing than someone else's case study.

I can't say this was the start of a beautiful friendship, but at least the adversarial nature of our interaction had softened. If Derek became an ally for increased safety, that was good enough for me.

## Epilogue

# It's still a program – not a project

Almost two years after Steve's accident happened and Dan's fall protection journey began, LMK Industries is still working to address its fall protection issues and advance its overall safety program. As Dan discovered at the beginning of his foray into fall protection, addressing these complex safety issues is never finished. It is an ongoing program that requires continuous attention and improvement.

The company hired Dan's preferred fall protection consultant to conduct a pilot fall hazard assessment and the first few phases of the existing system evaluation. The consultant is correcting problems and planning additional phases of the assessment and the evaluations. Serious progress is being made.

After proving his passion and aptitude for addressing fall protection issues, Dan transferred from his existing job into a full-time role in the safety department with the title of Fall Protection Champion. Pete still preferred to call him the Fall Protection Guru, but he eventually accepted the champion title. Together, Dan and Pete led the charge toward a more comprehensive managed fall protection program, modeled off the ANSI Z359.2 standard.

The employees recognized LMK's commitment to safety and the company's culture slowly shifted. Employees often brought up safety issues that were addressed quickly with help from supervisors and the safety department.

As Dan suspected, Ted became a strong advocate of the fall protection program on the management team. Derek remained skeptical, but was outnumbered on the management team and served as an important counterpoint on key safety issues.

Dan felt more fulfilled than ever in his job, and his family life with Cheryl and their daughters reflected his contentment. Dan's family still spent time with Steve's widow and her kids, although it became more difficult to do that as the kids got more involved in activities. Still, they never missed visiting Steve's gravesite together on his birthday and the date of his accident.

The last time they visited the cemetery, they brought flowers and shared a moment of silence. After that, Angela pulled Dan aside and said, "I truly believe that without your commitment to safety at the plant, there would be more tombstones for families to visit. Thank you for honoring Steve by devoting yourself to this cause. It really matters."

Angela's words kept Dan motivated and buoyed. One day, when the rigors of the job started to cloud his resolve, Dan received the following note in the mail:

Dear Dan,

I guess it's been over a year since we stopped working together, but I wanted to take a moment to let you know how much you influenced me. I don't think I even realized it at first, so I'm sure I never told you.

When we first started working together on the fall protection system at the site of Steve's accident, I didn't give much special thought to fall protection. It was just one of the many things I was supposed to understand and apply, but I only knew a little bit. Frankly, I treated the system at the accident location as just another project on my list of many to-do items.

Obviously, we found out you can't do that with fall protection. I'm so glad you stepped in and we had a chance to work together to make it right. I'm most proud of that, even though I didn't get it right until the second try when I began working with you.

I was inspired by the passion and commitment you showed to improving fall protection, and I learned a lot in the short time we worked together.

When I joined my new company, I had the opportunity to influence its entire safety program. I think the company was a little better at fall protection, but it still needed a leader and a champion to keep it going. With your influence, I dedicated myself to working on the fall protection program until it was right. We get high praise from the board, the community and our employees for our commitment to safety.

The real reason I'm writing to you is that we had a near-miss at our plant the other day. A worker fell, his fall was arrested, and he was rescued quickly. It was a scary incident for everyone involved, but everything worked the way it should and our employee went home that night unharmed.

I'm honestly not sure if that would have happened without your influence. Thank you for your commitment to improving fall protection and for willingly passing on that passion to others, especially me.

I wanted you to know that even though I'm working somewhere else, I am carrying the cause you so willingly took up in Steve's honor. So, the number of workers you've impacted with your commitment has doubled.

Thank you again for your excellent example. Keep up the good work. I know I will!

Sincerely,

Mark

# Resources

I hope this book has inspired you to learn more about fall prevention and protection, and how you can make a difference in protecting workers at heights. I invite you to seek out the following resources to learn more.

**LJB Inc.**
Website: LJBinc.com
Blog: thespot.LJBinc.com/category/safety/

**Occupational Health & Safety Administration (OSHA) Fall Prevention Campaign**
osha.gov/stopfalls/

**American National Standards Institute (ANSI) Fall Protection Standards**
asse.org/ansi/asse-z359-fall-protection-code-version-3-0-/

**American Society of Safety Engineers (ASSE)**
asse.org

**International Society for Fall Protection (ISFP)**
isfp.org

www.ingramcontent.com/pod-product-compliance
Lightning Source LLC
Chambersburg PA
CBHW022107170526
45157CB00004B/1526